OM KRISHNA I
Special Effects

OM   KRISHNA 1
Special Effects

Charles Henri Ford

Cherry Valley Editions

Printed by the Open Studio Print Shop (187 East Market
Street, Rhinebeck, N.Y. 12572), a non-profit facility for
writers, artists, and independent literary publishers,
supported in part by grants from the New York State
Council on the Arts and the National Endowment for the
Arts.

Library of Congress Cataloging in Publication Data

Ford, Charles Henri.
    Om Krishna I: Special Effects
    I. Title.
PS3511.039204   811'.5'2   78-16142
ISBN 0-916156-37-0 sgd. sp. ed. hdb.
ISBN 0-916156-36-2 pbk.

Photograph of author on page 60: On the occasion of his
poetry reading in Kathmandu 1973. USIS photo.

This book was made possible in part by a grant from the
National Endowment for the Arts, a federal agency, in
Washington, D.C., and in part by funds from the New York
State Council on the Arts.

Typeset by Ed Hogan/Aspect Composition
1105 Broadway, Somerville, Mass. 02144

Sections of this book were first published in Other Scenes (John Wilcock), Bastard Angel (Harold Norse), New Directions 23 and 35 (James Laughlin), SoHo News (Rochelle Ratner), Starstreams Poetry Series (Ira Cohen), Greek Heritage (Kimon Friar), Gay Sunshine (Winston Leyland), and in Americans Abroad (Lynne Tillman).

To Indra Bahadur Tamang
With love and gratitude

SPECIAL EFFECTS

I

Uncoiling coefficient imbued with trickster luster
My bulbous and prickly protégé sheds rings
    around us
Ask him to remove his photoelectric component
    holder
While we study the shrouded gall of thumbtack-
    making
Or attend classes in rolling friction
And throw away our begging bowls
According to spherical overtones
He runs hot-pressed wormwood through a stagger-
    fed vulcanizer
Seemingly unaware of half-elliptic reactors
He will pose for a likeness to be executed in fur-
    nace slag
On completion it is given eight passes through the
    Claes Oldenburg finishing mill
Sprayed with high temperature effervescence
It may con correspondents at the next Biennale
    and be offered to Peggy Guggenheim
Who will throw a shrinkage fit and file her nails
    with smyrna emery
With eyelid catalepsy she avoids the aborting of
    a ewe

*

Altered awareness assumes the jack-knife position
For elevator buckets and color amplifiers
The stinging hair of a sterile sunflower
(And cocaine ointment for cablecar modules)
Four large bundles from the royal vaults of China
Parachute to distant oases. Orphans advance, off-
    spring of the Dune Messiah
Reaching beyond the laboratory brain. The hermit
    of Upper Egypt
Counts Time's triangular pulse. Nandi crouching
    on a dais
Raises his head in adoration of the lingam
A portuguese commando in the ante-chamber
    wipes brick-dust from his eyebrows
The mystery is no mystery. Whatever you suppose
    him to be feeling he is feeling whatever reality
    you imagine is the reality
To transform the dreadful into the lyrical—what
    else is poetry, Rainer Maria

II

Trading with so much emergent sexology the Lis-
    tener bottomed out: 'A cloud is the top of a
    person you don't know is there.'
The shipping clerk added: 'Eulogize the un-
    squashed oyster. Feel it. It'll expand. Love
    is more healing than hallucenogenics.'
Lying in wait to eliminate the wild side rapid-
    loading elegance is keeping score. Sitting at
    her feet is history's poor cousin (underarm
    odor of stainless steel) a watcher of Eons

from the control tower of Chance. Between her legs: a slightly bitter bag, stitched with sparkling medalions.

Summer is learning! Keep a place for me. Call it black, sick, in, out, shocking, absurd... 'In this neighborhood, everybody has a gun.' The cultural renaissance, real New York style.

A makeshift adhesive, nameless procreation, descends like a backdrop. Last act nebula winging away from the highroad, it's the same oracularama. Foul-mouthed aristocrats give you the facts, like, man, the malodorous chainreaction from CIA files. Thrilling as the sight of a thundershower from the crosstown bus.

Stalled all day on a snowplough, the mayor sighed, 'May I be delivered from night baseball.' He's put his trust in stocks of invective. Emaciated panelists repeat a one-way paraphrase. Orthinologists agree, 'Most protoplasmic friction is pointless just the same.' Through the peepsight of retinal persistence everything is making it the piston-rod way.

So you want to be a pyromaniac, getting off his kernels in Potter's Field? No, you're not in Never Before, you're in Ever After. Hyacinthe is rocked by subtle sensuousness. Wheels go skimming in the Siberian moonlight.

III

With an elaborate wail
The womb strapped with Joseph Cornell
 anklets
Heads for the treasure seeker in the desert
An extraordinarily sophisticated inventor
In absolute control of time dissolves contra-
 dictory voices
And hallucinatory fugues
The moment they meet, vulture blooms hard-
 en into mother-of-pearl
Javelins of recording consciousness reach
 their overshoot

Like a suspicion of decompression-sickness
Blasphemies opulent as algae
Are quickly deciphered and as quickly for-
 gotten
On the borderland of transport they take
 leave of one another
The Shape—wire guided—at zero gravity
The Other, Ari Ho-chen, pocketing the per-
 fect title, There's a Vapor Dome on the
 Day Coach

IV

From the arsenal of incongruity any kind of mole-
 cules will do. My elephant driver's a self-
 service glacier, pining for liquefaction.
A cyclist approaching Vermilion Gulch puts his

finger on the master plan. Scraping pale carrots, misshapen as interbred penises, an extinct draftee wearing a bladder of moiré dances in the dugout. Inaudible as the interlacing roots of an artesian well, cyclonic as the absurd rhetoric of epic poetry, we rise... and dissect.

What did the moonmen call it? 'A woman needs two deodorants.'

Grandeur comes home.

*

Look, mommy, this girl is showing you what they are doing now. Oral copulation (a felony) and other pleasant things.

Because of the Yellow Peril's shrunken aggression (and because of its no-tangle wash-action) vapid numbers are carted out. One of the Lord's anointed becomes the Thing with fuzzy horns. In the cities of the demi-gods all men are born with charnel breeding powers.

Self-parody's the price of viscous rebound. In a slippery chase, to decide in which direction the razor-sharp heart will glide.

The puzzle of the piano in the Arab bazaar... Cloaked in sullen fallacy our superqueen takes a step towards bloodless gadgets. Panther coloring book teaches schoolkids to kill white pigs. Another snare to stunt the growth of timeless slavery. Toothpicks for the stray assets of existence.

V

Mysteries of behavior are solved by inanition
Not to act teaches us how to behave
Not to destroy shows us what to covet
A description of how you look becomes a work
    of art
You are the fortune one finds on a lonely road
    at night
Who is the rightful owner from whose groin do I
    gather you
Your sheen is not diminished, Sun-agate
Whose entrails are cloves and nutmegs

Let me stack the cards of enmity
Faint clues and indirections I trace out here
My intemperance is drawn to you
Nothing can ever deserve more than it deserves
I made an exception for myself without knowing it
You happened at the last moment like a rescue
I fly no prayer-flags we grow accustomed to
    amazement
I recognize you in the husk of what's to come

What should have dumfounded has made me
    eloquent
Fanged and glittering origin of orisons
I am familiar with every vile inch of you
Unfurl for me once more the prepuce of your lips
The impalpable is still in place

You give what is yours not to give
I am empty until you fill my incomparable senses
Standing inside the doorway as though desperate
Your lies are what give you away

VI

Arcane manoeuverings in a clouded-crystal ball...
Distended kickback of the quick-release
prong. Wrought-up pushovers require short-
er feeding periods.

When we analyze it, daily bread—that's what it's all
about. According to popular theory almost
everything we do is a game to overcome in-
stitutionalized irrationalities. A joy-knob
swim-through, in spite of yourself.

'I picked out this and that thing that interested
me, and then jumbled them in a bag... that's
not how to stake out a masterpiece—'

The lonely transvestite swooping across a mock
gun battle shines in the dark. All his bones
melt and he's a rippling waterfall of flesh,
tripping and burning while flicking sema-
phore messages to the imps of nostalgia.

'—But it's got your style, Ezra,'—and that's any
light rising in a supernatural harvest.

*

There's no turning back—so we thought. But how
high have you been? The best hope that cos-
mological exploration offers is this colossal

perversion of energy—it may awaken collec-
tive reaction to lift us from the jab-a-vein
causeway.

February 14th is a moldy fig in front. Chardo,
whip out your can of Pry-Fleet, squirt a
glob, smoothe it on and pow!. . . Pick of
the plush is not where we're going. Spring's
the time when mafia victims, dumped in
winter rivers, float to the surface.

Trendsetting in the name of high compliance,
when you've nothing to hide, there's no call
for wandering clumps of wierdos.

Manhattan Island is almost a foreign country. A
cracking galactic construction, with textured
pounces, communications failure and expen-
sive hookers.
'I didn't even realize that outer walls had
cavities.'

The weekend insurrectionists were surpassed by
trash in crummy hotels who inject mayon-
naise and peanut butter. ' 'Twas more rut
and pot-hole than shadow-play.'

Decadent American society plans to soft-land roses
by other names. Such splendors in the thin
Martian atmosphere may stir up the hornets
of Skyjack Heights.

Ah progress!

VII

This is the story of fire without flames
This is the plunge towards goals without honor

16

Halt, Messenger of Immortality
You in my arms it is myself I hold
My substance is upon you
A new name and I shall continue to exist
Placing my hand on yours I know reason and
    unreason
Idols on Obsession Avenue remind us of each
    other
Longing has nothing to do with knowing
Mothers of monsters you have seen yourselves
    give birth
Appearing and reappearing like any other excre-
    tion
I accept you without despite
The day I deceive you will bring truth to illusion
You disappear without having been deserted
I am glutted with your strangeness
Only part of you fits my idea of you
Into which of your eyes should I look
Now that I have given you pain I see you more
    clearly

VIII

Who threw a cloud up into the sky it's caught
    there clear-minded clear day it's just as well
    that all we dream isn't all that clear.
But don't count on a spokesman in the gutter to
    organize crack-ups. One way to do it is to
    toss off the hero.
Rundown words strike again. The sweetest will
    be answered, the sacrifice fits the punishment.

There it is now. . . a listening forest. Hope for a
        sniff of gentle water. And I went snarling on.
Crime is a protest, heartlessness the only morality.
Manjuri began to plow a furrow, having yoked a
        lion and a griffin. Dharma Sri Mitra went
        up to him and asked the way to Tibet. The
        mongoose on the postern turned back his
        eyes that he might not witness a fratricide.
Art is escape from estrangement, do children be-
        lieve? No they just play.

*

Sublunary suppuration with its hydrogen creep-
        in bogged down when court officials broke
        into the apartment where Miss Hazy Dream
        had barricaded herself. They confiscated a
        jasper necklace, two rings with seals, a silver-
        gilt chain with embossed emblem, a canvas
        suitcase with six cerulean and five beige
        blouses, two maxi evening dresses, and a
        round-trip glider badge. One mid-calf skirt
        from Patou, buttoned, slipped through the
        drain block.
'Don't twist my chain of paper towels!'
After the eloquence of a day of shame, old
        wounds testify. The blast from anywhere is
        a question of timing. When a scrubbed array
        of urchins refuses to be medically examined,
        learning - in - the - streets presides. Ideally,
        swine stomp together.

IX

Steel-clad hoisting ropes for heads of lard
Against the laws of mechanics
Counter irritants for bricklayers' itch
Vulcanized inhalers instead of mating gear
The reverse current is a quenching apparatus
Standing waves repay the pruning
Forestall feelings of tortion-tied tentacles

Cobra venom is a central acting drug producing
    euphoria
Rations of expansion are superimposed
Conduction bands bulge with beaver-tail castings
Under its influence a regression to infantile sexu-
    ality occurs
Bootstraps are four-stroke drop hammers
But psychopathic individuals are self-innoculated
When dream doors are unscrewed and removed
The ends of myth cycles are open to inspection
Glandular tubing is sucked to a ghastly headless-
    ness
On vertebrae tasseled with cleft lips
Explosion-proof emulsion registers gain
A composing room has been improvised in the
    caboose
Where a three-scoop banana split is melting
Auto-pollination is ruled out
But wrecking crews recover granulated asteroids
In the abcess, crystal violet with power to fertilize
We'll swob ourselves with a five-metal alloy
The blanking signals of design science are in flux

Parallel resonances set off voices in the playwright's head

On the emergency landing site tumescent spores are released

Analogous to the internal conversion of wild cow milking

X

At the start of the inventory foam-flakes scud along the oil slicks. Whoever works in close proximity to mindless skullbusters makes sure they never change.

Aware of an eventual pairing off, the charges stem from a fang-and-claw encounter. Top Knight strolled home lengths ahead of Uncertain Calm. In the equatorial boxcar a hint of the steepest antithesis.

'Taming the indiscernible' said Truman (Capote) 'as I grew older my unwillingness to be friendly toward men for my mother's sake kept recurring. Everyone knows I'm not traditional but I won't play it gay.'

Unlike a rancorous houseguest the refusal is pressed for time. Like treatment for hiccoughs it involves the interruption of the perpetuating reflex. It's all a mixable conservation.

Three six-footers circulating in the back—matted lashes and itching lids—paced to the vagaries of a Jacobean glossary. What else? A run on

the hypothetical library of our international
subculture—?

Golf balls with spikes, javelins made of snow-fence
slats, aerosol cans full of caustic oven-clean-
ing fluids, ice picks, clay tiles sharpened to
points that would have satisfied a Cro-Mag-
non spoor tracer. . .A put-upon housewife
was ultimately arrested for painting a four-
letter word on her forehead.

What about suits of armor? A dash of yearning
for community plates and fittings belongs to
woman-shaped women. Devastated begin-
ners a-gloat for tactical undress feel it.

Gibbering civilian you're all cramped up. Banish
the presbyterian ethic of work. For the mer-
cenary ready to retire, blinded by his own
racism, this is a message from his unstable
neighbor. You think the Kiss of Death is
exaggerated. Then you'll hardly make it
with a seven iron. So let the Hole in the
Ground tell you something.

All rooms are bedrooms.

XI

Protected by the mantle of the earth
Knowing that neither to lose nor to expect
Is to sail with sealed orders
We exhort him to ride by, intelligent sharpshooter
Blithe in the knowledge that our day has not
dawned

Horseman, resume your apocalyptic clacking
A rhythm to write a poem by, this sunset
Proving that what we say is not somnambulistic
Everything being the autobiography of music

XII

Tortured 9 years by 2 corns and a wart, the
Johnny Winter conspiracy rises to a fever
blister runaway. Trapped between amplifiers
the icecream cone renewal comes up ready
to blink. Light was meant to be!
Lord of total awareness, thug of self-effacing
porno violence, Horse of the Week, out to
get the adulation of millions, he's tearing
down prison terms, folks, in the public
interest.
It began with the heads. This blatant breed, with
civil disobedience, moves to the Times Square
Negro-White club. Would you call it a chaos
trip or a commitment that gits a little convul-
sive.
It's this way? What's that lump. Check it. We'll
buy the pie. The hunt's over.
Uppity, passionate as Byron, he has been called a
phenomenon. How come? Getting it is the
name of the Safety-pin.
Be thankful: surfers in giant screen can be fate-
ful too.
A social worker with hinged central divider for
cleavage bra, including lever-type cueing,
doubles as exerciser. The sweaty member-

ship, hot-back convention of smoldering incisions, leap-frog their way to rickety alcoves. Bring your armchair, partner, it's a cult revel for raunchy programers.

Polly Galvanick, 34, was formerly a deckhand, with full toss bronco muscles, called Flukey Sparks. Lonely and vulnerable, she changed her name after an operation in 1960. Right now she is very interested in Thomas Jefferson.

Jean-Luc to the rescue: 'It's strategic!' Like prerecorded variations appropriate to bombs on a train. Before his lecture series he mounted a unicorn stuffed with dollar bills and exclaimed, 'Chilled milk drinks should be sipped slowly and through a straw, comme dans les American drugstores!'

Hands resting on his lap, palm on palm, support a vase filled with the water of deathlessness. To be reborn as a human is not easy.

XIII

Metaphysical weasel may your firstborn inherit
The gift of escapades
Hallowed Hermaphrodite stymied in a unique
    progression
Peeling scorched vermin from your chestbone
Counterfeiter of chastity, you exude a special
    pungency
Kindness expires in the coils of concupiscence
Drives a stake through the heart of Orion

Haunted eyes encircle your every gesture
Diaphonous as words that define a heinous vow

XIV

A geek I know used to say that by standards pre-
     valent in gypjoint hospitals past and future
     have no meaning: they are merely 'in the
     dreaming'—
Get my brother-in-law: 'A girl's seldom too meek
     to learn about artificial insemination.' Sper-
     mobiles, triple-offer throwbacks... From the
     stiff in the photo-reconnaisance squadron:
     'Two of us still love each other.'
Vitriol on the mantlepiece, measure of the mauso-
     leum...
Throughout Galoot Wallow, in the acceleration of
     pretended rage, you'll see cars at night disper-
     sing bullets.   For the tub-of-guts nominee
     most of the git-along don't pay.
What's that making a pattern on our illustrious
     landmark?   A lyric soprano greaseball just
     left school.
Still scabrous scathing and scandalous Luis Buñuel
     is coming up the hill.   There's no reason to
     salute.   Living theaters are better suited to
     direct anguish.
'Space no longer exists,' according to the concep-
     tualist, rubbing a silver-coated plate, buffed
     and fumed with icy jade.
'Ambrosial split seconds have a way of fading,'
     said the sponge diver, redolent of swirls.

*

24

This Is About Me—to Gide.

Psst!   Morrison's pea-shooter is history running young.   He can't lose.   Baby-faced emptiness rearin' to go, hooray for inhibitions.

God-given form is far from bashful.   Properly conducted, the impatient hot dog begat blue meanies.

Oh la la.   He calls it joie de vivre.

Crime-fighting glamor boy, you haven't seen Chou En-lai's country of No Superstars.   Censors muffle a leader whose ideals slit, perforate, restore, enlarge, and seem to tangle with chicken 'n' dumplings.

Did you, mini-basket marauder, after that revolting song, keep biting even when bitten?

It would have paid you to tape it.

*

What's a baffled Marine resting in front of the Druid's Den for?   Brotherhood's too close to the roseate fan coral.

A hideous necktie in the lotus pond goes down.   Reminds me of some manic termite in a forgotten tea chest.   Narcotics of the sea, hurry up!

Surfacing in an amber spot the organic food shop on Washington Street is as far as you have to go.   Stocks conglomerate, oceanography and nursing-home issues are hit bad.   A burgeoning of temper tantrums, like in a naive unrealistic straight-cut movie.   Anyway it's time for

springing, covering, cushioning and 'Make
Me Unload.' Pop-Eye is going up on deck
to drop mescalin.
Who's calling please? If you're addicted you're
awarded a second dose. This is work?
Morning stiffness in three sizes pays off.
The complicated marriage of Venus, standing in a
canebrake with Long Crocodile, is part of the
equilibrium. Pickle Puss, singlehanded, won
a pack of sway-bait. On to Nadaville for
headless slashing, brash forerunner of the
workaday weed. To Bull's Bridge Bounce,
invading cascades and plazas...
The woman thing lies hidden until brought to a
pleasing and/or painful forcing of apertures.
If I owned an emporium for human oddities,
I'd show you Mistress Quickly socking it to
Adolph, who'd have loved a hero's funeral.

XV

Shuddering pageant, utter your joyous leaves
Untold apparitions dart out of themselves
Your thistles vibrate like halter-bells on a mule in
    some street in Iceland
Hooked hoods cruise in the starlight
A pennant of wretchedness fans the interchange
Of blessings incrusted with running sores
To cut into our bafflement a snake without mishap
Lunging at fugitives with 'face of oval scorn'

XVI

Poised as speedlight some word-blobs without punctuation to indicate stress are difficult to decipher. What became of Europe's finest non-iron sheets? Relentless wordmobiles make you wish for a few rest stops this side of catastrophe.

Since stealing a bike at the age of eight the Shiek of Esoterica is missing a ticket. Forming doubts about campy buttons a drifter out of silly old England soldiers with the slogan DOPE IS HOPE on his helmet. A fat-head organization approaches with the idea of importing replicas of the official 1969 inaugural medal. Buyers beware. Aesthetic convulsions are wrong again.

Socializing with O-fays is kept to a minimum at most Muslim resorts. Groups in clingy capes of Lumagard, a material containing phosphorescent pigment that absorbs sunrays during the day and, after nightfall, emits a whitish-green glow, balk at atonement. Daily briefings on Taoist scriptures will be followed by Seeing Things.

'Although the average door opens inward, your home would be better protected if you changed hinges.'

Dressed in chalk-white, pinching a tulip, Iggy laughed and said, I was just topsy-turvy... Black males respond differently to test anxiety than do black females. The black

man's self-image is less secure than the black
female's self-image. The black male tends to
be less achievement-oriented than do black
females. Black males of highschool age tend
to jeopardize the goal for immediate ego-
gratification.'
What's the connection between him and the
Harlem poor?
'I think yours is better made,' she said.
If that's what you've been exultant at, so you
drink it.
The classic shape is body and soul.

XVII

Loin de l'abbatoir plus doux que le sommeil
Tu te souviendra de mes manies atroces
Shrieks of loathing weave a web of ideal villainy
Faît-moi signe si tu veut te noyer
You attract by more than attraction through
ceaseless strings of bedevilment
A see-through parasite is sloping the other way
Eyelids open and close like Greek foreskins

XVIII

Scaley mammal lingering in what unreal quagmire
... Condemned to shadowy turmoil it's called
Retaliation Stench.
So far, the Yalta Conference quadrupeds, repul-
sively transfigured at every turn, talk only
about the semisolid uterus. Unavoidable as a

locust swarm, a destitute crew surrounds them.

'If Jehovah is to give us his vainglorious overhand, why not now?'

Fleas get thirsty on long trips. So does a misunderstood former child star. From this rewind her impersonation of a cave-dweller in sequined tulle will not be easily forgotten by Ursula Andress.

Subcutaneous tracery reappears. The tide of undesirables is rising, venereal linking with rustic tribesmen.

An unzipped vivisectionist finds himself aghast. In the zoological enclave, zealots in plum stockings try to save the situation.

What ecstatic straggler in arctic regions reaches out to hold me?

Tremulous profanation! Rain before eleven will set the right mood. During peak perturbation carnivores sneak home.

Agate-eyed Eros is sweeping the sidewalk. A sleepless stallion rotates in the archway.

XIX

Not to lose the drastic insight which is poetry
I spit words into hair hung with lice
The loot is signified by what it would conceal
Distilled birthmarks illegible regalia
Saying prayers in public places picking your nose
Hankering mystical a wrinkle across his stomach
    (wrinkle of youth)

He confers longevity on the sunset
The eyes of lost innocence grow luminous with
hate

Ask what the mountain asks
Waterfalls will answer when Antinous
Reading excerpts from A Season in Hell is saved
from self-destruction
The barking monkey-god cavorts with our faeces
Prostrate and gloating a pregnant sow foresees
the future
In the flung snot of princes

XX

The night patrol of the Afterlife opens a magneto
mouth—it's a piercing goodbye.
No sleeping pill freak he say 'I'll be there in a
minute...'
Let's enter one more wonderland of rapid re-
sponse. Suddenly it's so easy. He is not
alone—genius that creates where he was born.
Black is for HYPNOS, self-renewing flower of un-
censored fortune.
This is the other one, a suicide twin, the sun god
who one day may save your life!
Which one is sure he has it?
The clodhopper in a pleasure craft, willowy as
some of the world's best sailors, receives on
the rebound a touch of wireless paging.
Hold still, country bumpkin, while I change
your image to the supreme Androgyne.

30

Exulting in the shapeless fall of improvised bur-
　　dens we pay for effortless blot-out. Hand
　　grenades are not bracelets.
Behind the door marked Extermination, to be
　　truly loved is to be out of sight. Now you
　　know how not to behave peaceful. And to
　　witness without blushing the head-shaving
　　of Bottom Man Up on the sticky totem pole.
As the Ghoul enters the bedroom of Wolf's little
　　son, Peter, Viva Space-Mama flips flame-set
　　pinpricks from a motel-on-wheels.
That cold clear night, silky and poetic, she shot a
　　natural-born bore, clean legible form entitled
　　to its own zinc ointment. Sancta Simplicitas
　　blooms wild just once.
'To inherit you, generation of transplants, light on
　　yoga had to begin all over.'
O palest transport and perfectly realized breakout.
For satiny non-infectious toilet paper, the Com-
　　plete Plays of Racine.

XXI

We are the severings of a serpentine mirror
Reflections from nowhere the pieces grow to-
　　gether
Shake like thrones. Rampacious elephants
Display their imperceptible mobility
Exquisite in poverty rich robes hide you from as-
　　tonishment
Silverpoints of chiselled kneecaps screech like
　　avarice

Girls conscious of the virginity of boys increase
their pace
The lesson of being cornered: Get what you want
You have given everything: male jewels
The Goddess of Smallpox has not felt your face
Her kisses leave their identity
Another shadow edges towards the one I know
(What is less or more than a touch)
The jealousies you arouse, prongs in swamps of
radium
Carbon of arson a colon of tripe in the slot
machine
The sallow demeanor of a Prodigal Son
Mark the flora and fauna of a missing person

XXII

A well-conceived madonna is the eye-opening blur
of a gift-wrapped city.
Il Piccolo headed south, marching for a little
something more. Puny crooked boy god, he
goes by instinct.
But remember, mass conversion hum of ships
planes tanks and guns will be here soon, soon.
Philosophy's marathon hangup, dangling and
unwashed.

*

Open Letter from Vampire Land (written in in-
tegral diabolique).
The Disaster Area Look comes along.

Inside the Freezing Chamber, Roman Catholics remove their rubbers, qualify as Decency Rally delegates.

'This way!' Go in and find out what adrenalin recording does.

A Rolling Stone questionnaire to deviates from Deadlock, Nebraska revealed a shy defiance that invites a very blunt syringe. Miraculously clattering, they stay and sway in their own psychedelia. Uncle Meat is for the necrology room. The swing is to strong-arm floral arrangement and cephalic help for the degraded.

Don't get lost on Mars! One Rolls-Royce in the middle of Crater 13 bristles with arteries. It bumped into a sloop manned by repression robots.

Plugging abominable decals, blood bats loll about. The more you look, the more fierce the flesh.

Napoleon began the Battle of Waterloo at 11:30 A.M. Dracula carried the late Helen Chandler into the ruins of Carfax Abbey. For some ladies, there's a certain kind of abnormal lull, seems to nest in foldaway cruelties. It's the Mummy's Awakening Crawl.

XXIII

Beasts of song unstring their priceless tokens
Pearls for Verlaine to dissolve on his tongue
An opal for Oscar to throw at the feet of the

Sphinx
And for the one whose smile never closes, the lip-
  less one
Rising and falling in a danse macabre
Un collier des flammes sinistres
Comme le lyrisme elle vous prendra par la gorge
Bandages of cunning bind the werewolf in the
  ravine
Excavated yesterday catatonically posed
He is being found out for what he is
My double in a martyr's stranglehold
Bruised and unmalleable droppings
Fit stomach ligaments somber to behold
(Faded gardenia of figurative unfoldings)
Halting at the sight, la belle dame sans merci
Feels only irritation at bungled suicides
I snip the code-shaped coverings knowing you for
  the ostentatious cripple
Who will banish my distrust of alien broods

XXIV

Take-over remains in Texas. Copper values jump.
  A girl manacled north of Doohickey fails to
  spot miscreants on the road to Elemental
  Rapture. 'I saw a Columbia records adver-
  tisement right next to a description of a
  blow-job. I wonder where the ticks go in
  wintertime.'
Raquel Welch, big name in excess baggage, has se-
  lected John Drew Barrymore for the lead in
  No Place For The Dead, which she is produc-

ing independently. He will be given cold baths and then made to stand naked beside open windows. Youth troops storm in, to confront a woman deeply troubled since losing touch with her teenage son's life pattern. 'The Pentagon has seen fit to put him in the Seventh Fleet and he is not considered mature enough to have a corrugated monster suit.'

Bathtub users must look to the right and to the left before getting into the tub. They must calm down when reaching for a washcloth or a bar of soap, and they must learn to be ready for the unexpected when they are rinsing off. The psychiatrist in charge of the locker-room line-up found a dry hole for the wrong wavelength. If you kick the dispenser at the top of Kensington Street you get free milk. Elsewhere, the flag is stiffened with wire. Don't touch!

A strapped-down Aztec hungers for Ringo. Link-up spittle as an end in itself.

Following thick-skinned summit meetings at overseas bases Dragon Puss putting the heat on reveals one of the tricks of emotionalism: the free world brandishing purchase coupons.

There's the captain. After he burns back issues of Monster News in People's Park (a whiff of teargas in the dawn is unlike any other micromirage) it not only arouses a Cosa Vol Dire outcry, like the squalor of the First Children's Crusade, but the patron saint of

Jackson, Mississippi lashes out ruthlessly too.
Born-to-kill Steve McQueen deals with the
youngest of the Frankensteins:
'If you play, you pay, but if you lose your cool
you get screwed.'
Negotiation in a house of worship?   Close the
pump.   Loco Puertoricans in a downhill
stopover redeem a brother under pressure.
Spurting a sheen from anywhere adjustment
school creep operates eye-level prism. There's
always a pusher—cutting deep to suit the
blight.
No one does it like an aching kid, looking for a
place to stay.

XXV

Two imbeciles are digging a grave for the heredi-
tary emperor
Owls will prophecy upon it
Ribald ballerinas rehearse diabolical ballets
Far from the coastline, playing with sand
Fond expressions sprout like pygmies
With no given letters to absorb
Until the snow tigers melt at the crossroad of the
Blessed Sphincter
Twitching with languor I stumble upon a first line
Enamored of the rumblings you encase
As if you were a half-crushed frog in saline
solution
Living statue whose bodily complexion is a white
island in an ocean of milk

XXVI

Alchemists shift the unadulterated. 'Testing 1-2-3
. . .' Persuasive jargon gets through. Wrap-
around friends intensify the trajectory. 'Slide
your eggs into the middle of the capsule!'
Daughters such as Diana, flamboyantly hunting,
intercept wonders. Staccato yellow animals
watch, wide-eyed and earthy.
Childbirth in the classroom is always a welcome
break. What's happening in Wenceslas Square
today?
'We call it sonic flare—sensitive to a certain dazzle,
and when the network is struck the rapidity
is a large comb.'
A post-grad stud, sought on charges of failure to
keep drugs in the original container, whizzed
round the corner carrying fragrant Scottish
roses.
Brainwork's a spooky thing, the way traveling
should always be.

*

Clue to a hogfest, as told to our slob in Tangier.
The purse-snatching ideologue, renowned for
Anna May Wong charme et beauté, spreads
his scrotal sac (white supremacy where it
really hurts).
No one can revile with a plastic heart. In a for-
mal dinner jacket every doctor would look

like Gore Vidal (author of Myra Brecken-
ridge) at a loss for words.
That's the genius of the Great Ritual. 'It's com-
petitive!' A popular expression meaning
heaven on earth.
But Shelley, seeing what he wanted to see (inter-
com thralldom) had the look and feel of a
turned-on co-pilot.
Nor could snatch impersonation have created a
distress signal. A 12-year-old cock looks
lovely by candlelight. In the background,
portrait of an electric toothbrush.

XXVII

Dehumanized sentences teach him everything
The touch of budding leaves, color of the inner
thigh
He was scratching with the nails of parakeets
At the age of thirteen his two arms and chest as-
sumed heraldic comeliness
'This man-child has reddish lumina in seven places'
Three parts of his body are short: the neck fore-
arms and genitals
Fate lines on his palm: a flag, wheels, a thunder-
bolt and a fish
Impetuous as freedom from all unwanted occu-
pations
He has an inconceivable lack of dormant egotism
While a heron imbibes falling water, water as it
falls from a rain cloud
Butter is smoothed on his face. He was sleeping

in the ecstasy of ghastliness
Trapped within his mother (a mess of urine and
    liquid stool)
Unable to control the two welts that were his lips
He was merged in seas of imponderable goodness
Another example of indirect carnage
Let us imagine that we have imagined it all.

XXVIII

And now, wanna hear my stereo recording of It's
    Not How Long You Make It, It's How You
    Make It Long—? You have nothing to lose
    but your garters. La commedia è finita! Cut
    to Walt.
Boys 11-16, guilty of consentual sodomy, shut
    off the alarm. Will you be one of the privi-
    leged to share in this unique experience?
    Mucho fun!
'I set my hair with bobby pins. How can I prevent
    ridges from forming?'
Shut your eyes to the shame. Sado-masochistic
    fans do it. Like the way eight live lobsters
    push during take-off. Wash your love cir-
    cuits, little fellows.
Enfin, who's Americanized? 'Man, it's dogshit.'
Mrs. Kana Kogi, a 4th degree black-belt karate
    master, can easily crack a cocoanut with one
    swipe. Go ahead, lady. After napalm, there's
    more hip room. Thank heavens for a Negro
    view: 'You've come... baby.'
Behind the quest for extinction there's a desperate

mystique. True octagonal hex springs up in
blind alleys. On the outskirts of Plunderers'
Realm there's a mental hospital where Ariadne
checked in. Her looney guru argued, 'You
must face the ordeal of a growing heart.'

XXIX

Put your trust in me I shall be inspired by false-
        hood
My awkwardness only makes you more graceful
To deny is to embrace without possessiveness
If tomorrow you are the same I shall await the
        day after
Your teeth are white as white radishes
Before you wore these clothes they were not holy

In the slough of intolerable autumn you are the
        deprivation I can least afford
The invisible is what we cherish most
Unearthly and collapsible
I am not certain of your ferocity
What would we do without our deceptions
We are the childless children of ourselves

XXX

Churning mist like island twilight the voyage of
        the Pythagoras begins
'I think one of the seamen last night said, Jesus
        Christ was a bad motherfucker!' No threat

to sopping sleeping bags.

As removed from evil as a bus stop in Claygate, guerilla cubs are clannish unbending cherubs. They throw off their clothes in front of any mob, especially at a concert, revelling in public nakedness. Enjoyable perhaps as the brainwashing of Arabs. First, two boys are made to live in the same room with an older Israeli girl. Naturally they compete for her attention, but whenever one of them thinks he has won her friendship, the girl is changed. The whole process is repeated several times, a malevolent pantomime. Do you have what she holds? One of them is ours.

Deadpan decrepitude, get out of the way! In a crapper society, for fatherly off-color things to do, once more our slimy running mate, flinging unbuttoned and immodest shit, inaugurates a mock-heroic portfolio.

I don't care if you speak executive mansion gibberish, Iwo Jima got enough. Getting stuck rates a Texas-size crybaby.

See how they ball! Like a schizoid scoutmaster swallowing you up.

What's wrong? You get what you spit on. Lovelorn fellatio makes no noise. Self-centered cunnilingus, It's your move.

According to latest U.S. Government figures the nonconforming sun, turbulent as a diamond (or a dragqueen in a pigsty) hardly needs Symbolism, the disease that became the core.

Parrots veer from the alphabet straight into a
   fly-paper tambourine.
Powerless as an atheist in a painted tabernacle the
   Dali-esque fright bride overreacted, helped
   reverse a tentative togetherness. 'Take me to
   your wasteland dining pit, where empire
   builders smash their cold-drawn formulas!'
To Sophocles a young boy's kisses were sweeter
   than spring onions. Shakespeare liked to be
   fucked in the woods.

XXXI

To turn failure into success
Think of the odyssey of an untraceable pugilist
For instantaneous malperformance
The well-known variation of the Semislav Defense
To slow the spread of multinationals
Polar conversion and mental disorders of machines
With Stellarator C under construction
Urban sprawl is fully shared by the onlooker
Though we may never guess who the heroine is
The validity of sensuality is beyond dispute
Like two cars burning together after a head-on
   collision
The process of continuing to write poems may be
   equated
With bones shedding their crustacean armor in an
   opalescent vacuum
Though at times analogous to an extravaganza in
   a re-entry vehicle

XXXII

Aren't you glad that sooner or later we was born.
That means never again.
So don't try to wake me up when you can have
    forever.
Nobody's fooling—my world just growed.
In a second it's that same old cop-out, strictly
    insane, want to sell you all or nothing.
And the Hong Kong flu lasted too long.
My father at his best figured out some things.
When it's over they'll connect.
It's hard to kick education, anything good that
    was almost mine.
It still can be the greatest, I could hit it and be a
    winner.
But that was me who flunked today.
The last rules have been broke, like by the Wizard
    of Who.
He not the first magician to frighten and heal.
No point in anybody else's wish—too bad we don't
    all grows up cool.
What I want so much, start a big noise somewhere.
And for good measure to look prettier.
Girls arent very helpful, just here to cover you up.
And that's what I call stupid.
Cinderella means you'd never guess what.
She sleeps around. . . and we think that's messy.
I've got to write a fan letter to that lady in the
    window putting on a show.
I wouldn't miss Jerry Lewis starring in Who's

Minding the Store.
But most of all I need a invitation.

XXXIII

The will to change is effort wasted you don't
    choose your roles they choose you
'The more you kill the more you gain'—but only
    for as long as a mustard seed can stand up-
    right on a cow's horn
I am the coherence I don't care what *you* are I
    only care if I love you
To suck your tongue (unmelting strawberry) the
    stones of memory are the ones that sprout
A bafflement of meanings
But the human all too human is always ordinary
Accidents of proximity create our lives
Beauty gets its way ugliness has to pay
          And the birds of paranoia
          Twitter at dawn
          But we have already listened to them
          All night, in our dreams
Hendrix busted in Toronto. . . He's not the only
    maharajah wears bonnets of the unbelievable

XXXIV

'A poisoned arrow, getting in the mood!'
The standard of an albino archer includes an ice-
    age snout. Prufrock, withered adversary,
    steps down. From his warehouse of disin-
    fected altarcloths, hatchet-man swirling back-

44

wards, he flays at feathery portals. A flaw in his bullet-making blueprint confers a bloodless murmur.

Beginners in segregation bastinade the embers, disembowel anagrams. From the Sea of Boneless Craving a dismantled pouch has reached the Earth.

Asleep in a rectangle of phosphorescence the uncircumcized apostle gives a countersign.

It takes degradation, Etruscan style, to ken the markings of a fag-end existence.

Against the snow-cloud, an apple-green aquarium.

XXXV

To the hounding image: the prey we prefer is the Self
Anointed with oils from your pores
Any finger's worth will swell my beatitude
It is the non-odor of Sansara
Near where my tongue struggles
There where you've not felt it before
I also delight in your discolored lower teeth
Your neck is stalwart and needs scrubbing
Be careful of diseases without titles
And eyes alive with truth and untruth
Flaking hollows Aeolian chimes
You could be anyone no plea has produced you
The purity of solitude is unaffected
You perform a contract with my fate
Perfection invites catastrophe I am convinced of nothing

The Jesus of beauty is a prostate gland
Gems that spring from one dark to another
The most precious of the precious never see the
    light

Prickly head flushed with corpuscles
My life made complicated by your simplicity
Ignorant of the end he knows the Way
We do not break the rules of others
We are our own outlaws

XXXVI

But how describe a cobweb clinging to the Great
    Wall of Schizophrenia... Its whole purpose is
    to give out a half-nameless clutch, limiting
    the sensibility. Innate waste has it, scraggy
    as a freak-out with farwest drive, high veloci-
    ty recipe for illustrious sabotage.
A half-wit's found in the patio. The compulsory
    lanterns of ourselves have been taken down.
O floundering predilections of my mediumistic
    chimera.

XXXVII

Skinning back the living teeth of Asia
It will rain all night I said
My love may not be pure but it is complete
And poetry is a lyric wisdom or it doesn't last
A quiet dawn and sleep in the body asks, 'What
    have you done to me?'

Lovers with nacreous longhis are trapped in their
    loggias
With houses as with people, you love them you
    use them you leave them
Who belongs most to which
Writing comes out, aura to attract no one for there
    is no one to attract
Sway, banana leaf, I too am swaying I know how
    you feel
Living as though we had all the time in the world—
    and we had, and we have

XXXVIII

Flame-thrower at eventide, pied with gossamer tis-
    sues. . .Outpost ulcerations have survived.
    Hothouse appendages appear. In the gloam-
    ing, the excavation of a 1932 luncheonette.
Languishment-speckled gratification. . .like a con-
    vent quickening with roaches and handjobs.
On the esplanade, inflammable plumage of silent
    insolence is flaunted by a wading bird.
Inside the tilt-table room for physiological prob-
    ing, handcuffed with an amulet Valentino's
    valet dropped on the floor of the deadletter
    office, there's a bucktoothed child bride. On
    her lips, color of grasshoppers' eyes, the taste
    of codeine. Her dazed and unsure abductor,
    decoder of benedictions, no sooner has it out
    than an amphibian in dungarees deploys noc-
    turnal emissions on a rhythmic scale.
On the dancefloor of fractured glass, locomotives

of unutterable glut. . . O incoherent after-
birth!
But hands off the eight-legged day laborer. There's
still the asexual clot to be recycled. Antagon-
ist composed of fiery substances, he'll tell
you about chemical toilets and the only
spectrographic lab this side the creamery.
The Pope is about to visit Africa, to mourn an en-
gulfed battalion and to purchase footspray
for airtight confessionals.
A hairy veil hangs over the unexplored Atlantic.

XXXIX

Recollected in tranquility: Addio to the Duke
What is your color? Sapphire-black)
The tolltaker was stabbed
Men are easier to kill and eat than tame cattle
A tongue of the remorseless riptide
Taught him the art of significant gesture
Language net, I cast you wide
Hoping to retrieve a few emeralds of insanity
('. . .for there are scenes that call for strange fare-
wells')

Filthy surgeons with criminal connections climb
ladders of smoke
Sapphire-black I reclaim you on the brink of shriek
Whole bananas not just peels are in the aisles
All the mistakes have at last been made and there
are none left to make

But the unvanquished sun whips the blood
Engendering giants of the incalculable
Leaving in their wake an aftersense of spasms of
    awareness

EPILOGUE: FIVE ELEGIES

ENSHRINED

Picking the locks of fire-opals with a feather key

The most beautiful the least dangerous is on stage
center

With her garnet-studded fleshing knife

Palmo is removing hair, fat and loose skin

Ripping open the abdomens of three pregnant
women, taking out the foetuses

She committed her first murder at the age of
twelve

At fourteen she preferred licking blood from
thorns—her own blood

Honey in the mouth razor at the belt she secured
her crimes with greater crimes

A photo of the poète maudit—the only one,
Rimbaud—she wears in an onyx locket

With shield-shaped motorcycle gloves, piercing
clouds of ice-dust leading to temples of hor-
ror

Face-cutter of unimaginable contrivances

She may be neither created nor destroyed

Mixed with burnt shells and white of egg closed
circle

Of squirm and splash poignant and impassive her
name is Zina Rachevsky

MISHIMA

The unplayed idea returned to haunt you, Yukio
    Mishima
Walking wounded with that deadly merchandise,
    your mind
A poem is only a poem, it can't be anything else
    you said
And then turned your thoughts to something else,
    more emotional than cerebral
A furious abortion in a Prague suburb perhaps
Or a prisoner used as guinea pig
The unguarded revelation is the one you never shot
    down

To limit the chance of counterattack
You pretended to be asleep when the dragon
    breathed fire
Carrying in your pocket always the rarest of even-
    tualities
Actually you were more attracted to power than
    to people or to art
Your underlying drive chameleon-like shifts in
    strategy
And now wherever you go, accompanied by minors
    ('they don't answer but they listen')
You wear the hidden smile that triggers the trance
    of the sun

MAX ERNST

Though the practice of chastity confers magical
   powers
The yoga of the uncreated will leave you on a
   flame-like plateau
Hernando's situation was hopeless
His skull fractured and his clothes on fire
The rear tire of his Yamaha torn to shreds
The attempt to persevere in solitude had come to
   this
Speeding from all the animistic taboos which had
   been broken and which had broken him
The absolute spectral response is addictive
And though his correction fluid came through
   with a finishing spurt
The distortion was demonic
At one time he was the fastest of humans
Sprinkled with camphor dust he made the last
   energy transfer
Was it all due to a weakness on the dark squares
Or to antibodies delicate and frightening as a throat

ST.-JOHN PERSE

Holding habit-shaped memories in a leopard-skin
    apron
The bone of your left ear vibrating to stars of
    deep seas
Saint-John Perse prisoner on a lost planet
You dreamed of other existences
Had it been the wandering spirit of a jungle fighter
Who entrusted you with the ignition key to the
    wheel of truth
You may have discarded the ten causes of regret
But you were a sky-goer
And paid homage to a dragon-headed moon
Installed on the lion-throne

At the cremation grounds where, cotton-clad, we
    attended your last rites
Gods of the world of formlessness
Were there to participate in the mystic drama
In your ashes I sensed no cessation of thought
Your meanings, apparitional and boundless, added
    up to the sacred number 7

CANDY DARLING

'. . .the death, then, of a beau-
tiful woman is unquestionably
the most poetical topic in the
world. . .'
          — Poe

The King of the Monkeys tried to marry her
As though he had not been upset enough in his
    life she was eager to upset him more
From the nursery of murderers he led you to the
    golden dustheap
Entering a supersensual universe spun by the
    human spider
You stood by a window framed with dogwood,
    just to prove the folly of a diamond-tipped
    blade
I saw the fiendish treatment you gave to a young
    pearl
To identify the opposites of an artificial order a
    dwarf was sewn to your abdomen with se-
    cret threads
Bereft of origin and change wrapped in wire cloth
    white hard but malleable they buried you
    in the skin of a black deer

To small heartless caterpillars you are the sorcer-
    er-saint dissolving in star-showers
Exquisite aberration, the garment of decay was
    not for you
Like an upside-down butterfly or a man without
    eyebrows in all that rushing annihilation

yours was the historic aura of a peacock's
grace
You went as a stranger where strangers go, bro-
ken crescent in a sky of enigmas
Moonlit birds have alighted holding a rosary of
human teeth in claws of bright benevolent
steel
I lift the glass of veneration to a glimmering vi-
sion, explosive flower planted in the mud of
a lawless world

CHRONOLOGY

1913 - Born February 10, Brookhaven, Mississippi.

1929 - Dropout from High School, started little mag *Blues,* Columbus, Miss.

1931 - To Paris and the salons of Gertrude Stein, Natalie Barney, Marie-Louise Bousquet. Became friends with Man Ray, Kay Boyle, Janet Flanner, Peggy Guggenheim, Djuna Barnes and others of the Expatriate colony in Montparnasse and Saint-Germain-les-Près.

1932 - To Morocco, lured by Paul Bowles' glowing accounts. Joined there by Djuna Barnes; typed for her the novel she'd just completed, *Nightwood.*

1933 - *The Young and Evil*, novel written in collaboration with Parker Tyler, published by Obelisk Press, Paris; banned in England and America.

1934 - Return to New York, bringing Pavel Tchelitchew. The milieu was Carl Van Vechten, Glenway Wescott, George Platt Lynes, Lincoln Kirstein, Julien Levy, Orson Welles, George Balanchine, Cummings, Ruth Ford —et al., augmented by visiting friends-from-overseas: Cecil Beaton, Leonor Fini, Hoyningen-Huene, Dali, etc.

1938 - First full-length book of poems, *The Garden of Disorder,* introduction by William Carlos Williams.

1940 - ABC's—poem with Joseph Cornell collage cover. Started *View,* which evolved into the magazine that advanced the European artists in New York (who were to influence the art scene in America): Tchelitchew, Tanguy, Ernst, Masson. View Editions, during the Forties, published first monograph on Marcel Duchamp and first book translations of André Breton's poems.

1941 - New Poems, *The Overturned Lake,* with Matta's title page and frontispiece.

1949 - New Poems, *Sleep in a Nest of Flames,* with Edith Sitwell's preface.

1952 - To Europe with Tchelitchew, constant companion since 1934 (a relationship that was to end only with Tchelitchew's death in Rome, 1957).

1955 - Thirty Images from Italy, exhibition of photographs at London's Institute of Contemporary Art.

1956 - First one-man show of paintings and drawings, Paris, catalog foreword by Jean Cocteau.

1962 - Return to U.S.A. Period of association with Pop artists and underground filmmakers.

1965 - Poem Posters, exhibition at Cordier & Ekstrom gallery, triggered color-poster explosion. Film made of this show chosen for Fourth International Avant-Garde Film Festival, Belgium.

1966 - *Spare Parts*—'artist's book' produced in colorphoto-litho, Athens, Greece.

1968 - *Silver Flower Coo*—collage poems. (Looks "like no other book ever published in

America"—Richard Kostelanetz.)

1971 - New York premier of feature film, *Johnny Minotaur,* 'conceived, directed and photographed by Charles Henri Ford on the Island of Crete.'

1972 - *Flag of Ecstasy*—Selected Poems.

1974 - The Kathmandu Experience: exhibition at the New York Cultural Center of works created in Nepal: wood sculptures, wall hangings, prints.

1976 - Postcards to Charles Henri Ford: exhibition of 108 postcards from friends over a 25-year period.

1978 - *Om Krishna,* volume one in a tetralogy of new poetry.

Set in Baskerville and printed on Warren's Olde Style on the Heidelberg Kord at the Open Studio Print Shop, this first edition consists of 1,000 copies of which 100 are handbound by Alan Brilliant of Unicorn Press, with an original photograph by the author.

$3.50
CHERRY VALLEY EDITIONS
Box 303,
Cherry Valley,
NY 13320